THE GREAT BIBLE

Discovery

JERUSALEM REBUILT - EZRA AND NEHEMIAH

THE BIBLE IS A BEST-SELLER. IT IS ALSO ONE OF THE MASTER-WORKS OF WORLD LITERATURE - SO IMPORTANT THAT UNIVERSITIES TODAY TEACH 'NON-RELIGIOUS' BIBLE COURSES TO HELP STUDENTS WHO CHOOSE TO STUDY WESTERN LITERATURE.

THE BIBLE POSSESSES AN AMAZING POWER TO FASCINATE YOUNG AND OLD ALIKE.

ONE REASON FOR THIS UNIVERSAL APPEAL IS THAT IT DEALS WITH BASIC HUMAN LONGINGS, EMOTIONS, RELATIONSHIPS. 'ALL THE WORLD IS HERE.' ANOTHER REASON IS THAT SO MUCH OF THE BIBLE CONSISTS OF STORIES. THEY ARE FULL OF MEANING BUT EASY TO REMEMBER.

HERE ARE THOSE STORIES, PRESENTED SIMPLY AND WITH A MINIMUM OF EXPLANATION. WE HAVE LEFT THE TEXT TO SPEAK FOR ITSELF. GIFTED ARTISTS USE THE ACTION-STRIP TECHNIQUE TO BRING THE BIBLE'S DEEP MESSAGE TO READERS OF ALL AGES. THEIR DRAWINGS ARE BASED ON INFORMATION FROM ARCHAEOLOGICAL DISCOVERIES COVERING FIFTEEN CENTURIES.

AN ANCIENT BOOK - PRESENTED FOR THE PEOPLE OF THE SECOND MILLENNIUM. A RELIGIOUS BOOK - PRESENTED FREE FROM THE INTERPRETATION OF ANY PARTICULAR CHURCH. A UNIVERSAL BOOK - PRESENTED IN A FORM THAT ALL MAY ENJOY.

OM publishing
CARLISLE, UK

16

Unlike the Assyrians and Babylonians, the Persians organized their empire efficiently. From the time Cyrus allowed the Babylonian Jews to return to Jerusalem, Judah was part of the Persian province 'Beyond the River [Euphrates]', ruled by a non-Jewish governor.

The first group to return (in about 537 BC) found the city and the Temple in ruins. It was not until 520-515 that the Temple was rebuilt, thanks to the encouragement of the prophets Haggai and Zechariah. When we remember how the earlier prophets had warned their hearers that the Lord was not chiefly interested in sacrifices we may be surprised that these prophets should attach such importance to rebuilding the Temple. But in the new situation, the Temple was a sign that the little community in and around Jerusalem was still loyal to the God of Israel.

Another thing that bound them together was obedience to the law of Moses. This is why it was such an important development when Ezra was sent to be in effect Commissioner for Religious Affairs in Jerusalem. From this time, the law of Moses was to be the official law of Judah.

Another Jew sent to Jerusalem with imperial authority from Susa, the Persian capital, was Nehemiah. From 445 to 433 BC he was the Governor. He organized the life of the city and saw to the rebuilding of the walls. When he returned to Jerusalem some years later, he took action against those who were harming the life of the community.

These years saw the beginning of Judaism, with its emphasis on racial purity and strict obedience to the Law. No longer a kingdom, the nation's only hope lay in the coming of the messiah. When disasters struck them, such as the droughts and plagues that led Joel to prophesy, they saw them as a sign of the Day of the Lord. At the same time, they looked forward to a transformed creation, a time when God would pour out his Spirit on all his people, men and women, young and old.

HAGGAI	ZECHARIAH
MALACHI	EZRA
NEHEMIAH	JOEL

JERUSALEM REBUILT
EZRA AND NEHEMIAH

First published as *Découvrir la Bible* 1983

First edition © Larousse S.A. 1984
24-volume series adaptation by Mike Jacklin © Knowledge Unlimited 1994
This edition © OM Publishing 1995

01 00 99 98 97 96 95   7 6 5 4 3 2 1

OM Publishing is an imprint of Send the Light Ltd.,
P.O. Box 300, Carlisle, Cumbria CA3 0QS, U.K.

Introductions: Peter Cousins

British Library Cataloguing in Publication Data
A catalogue record for this book is available from the British Library
ISBN 1-85078-220-2

Printed in Singapore by Tien Wah Press (Pte) Ltd.

THE REBUILDING OF THE TEMPLE

THIS IS WHAT CYRUS, THE KING OF PERSIA, SAYS: THE LORD, THE GOD OF HEAVEN, HAS ENTRUSTED ALL THE KINGDOMS OF THE EARTH TO ME, AND GIVEN ME THE TASK OF BUILDING HIM A DWELLING-PLACE IN JERUSALEM.

BY THE BEGINNING OF THE YEAR 538 B.C., CYRUS HAD ALREADY BEEN KING OF BABYLON FOR SEVERAL MONTHS.

...ALL OF YOU WHO ARE HIS PEOPLE, ARE FREE TO GO BACK TO JERUSALEM AND REBUILD HIS HOUSE.

THIS TIME IT IS TRUE! WE CAN GO BACK!

I WAS BORN HERE; I DON'T WANT TO LEAVE.

SCENARIO: Etienne DAHLER
DRAWING: Carlo MARCELLO

BUT, CYRUS, WHY ARE YOU BEING SO KIND-HEARTED?

IF YOU MAKE PEOPLE AFRAID, YOU REAP HATE... BUT IF YOU TREAT THEM WELL, YOU REAP...

LOVE! THAT ISN'T TOO STRONG A WORD... CYRUS, THEY LOVE YOU LIKE A FATHER!

JERUSALEM! AT LAST WE'RE GOING BACK TO JERUSALEM! AFTER SO MANY YEARS!

AFTER ALL THE LOOTING THERE CAN'T BE MUCH LEFT!

IT IS ALL VERY WELL TO GO BACK THERE, BUT HOW WILL WE LIVE?

IF YOU DON'T TRUST GOD, STAY HERE! WE DON'T NEED YOU!

LED BY **JOSHUA**, THE HIGH PRIEST, AND **ZERUBBABEL**, WHO HAD BEEN APPOINTED GOVERNOR OF JERUSALEM, SEVERAL THOUSAND PEOPLE SET OFF...

WE'LL FOLLOW YOU SOON...

AT THE BEGINNING OF THE YEAR 537 BC, EVERYTHING WAS READY FOR THEM TO LEAVE BABYLON. THE HOLY VESSELS FROM THE TEMPLE, WHICH NEBUCHADNEZZAR HAD TAKEN IN 587, WERE HANDED BACK TO **ZERUBBABEL**, GRANDSON OF JEHOIACHIN.

IT TOOK THEM NEARLY FIVE MONTHS TO WALK TO THE HOLY CITY, STILL UNDER PERSIAN RULE.

GRADUALLY THOSE WHO HAD COME BACK, BEGAN TO WORK ON THEIR FARMS...

NOW THAT WE HAVE SOMETHING TO EAT, WE CAN GET ON WITH REBUILDING THE TEMPLE.

ABOUT TIME, TOO! WE'VE BEEN BACK FROM BABYLON FOR TWO YEARS!

THE RUBBISH WAS CLEARED FROM THE RUINS OF SOLOMON'S TEMPLE. THE HOLY SQUARE WAS UNCOVERED...

... AND A LITTLE WHILE LATER THE FIRST STONE WAS LAID.

BLESSED BE THE LORD, THE GOD OF ISRAEL...

...BECAUSE HIS LOVE LASTS FOR EVER!

AND NOW? WHY ARE YOU CRYING, GRANDDAD?

I SAW SOLOMON'S TEMPLE! ... BELIEVE ME, YOUNG MAN, THIS ONE WILL NEVER BE AS SPLENDID!

HEY, SIMEON, AREN'T YOU GOING TO WORK ON THE TEMPLE?

ALL MY WORKERS HAVE LEFT! SO... BREAD FIRST!

THERE ARE HARDLY ANY WORKERS HERE, AND YOU CAN'T EXPLAIN IT?

NOW I UNDERSTAND... OBVIOUSLY SIMEON ISN'T THE ONLY ONE LEFT BY HIMSELF...

VERY SOON THE WORK ON THE TEMPLE STOPPED ALTOGETHER ...

THEY WERE JUST AS SUCCESSFUL WITH THE PERSIAN OFFICIALS...

RIGHT YOU ARE! WE'LL HAVE MORE CONTROLS... THE CONVOYS BRINGING MATERIALS WILL BE SLOWED DOWN.

THIS IS ALL YOUR FAULT, ZERUBBABEL! YOU DON'T KNOW HOW TO DEAL WITH THE SAMARITANS... WHAT'S MORE, THAT IS MY JOB, NOT YOURS!

BUT, JOSHUA, WHO IS GOVERNOR HERE?

EXCUSE ME, BUT... THE PERSIAN GOVERNOR WANTS TO SEE YOU.

WHO? ME?

BOTH OF YOU!

THE YEARS WENT BY. IN 529 BC CYRUS DIED, AND HIS SON CAMBYSES BECAME KING.

EIGHT YEARS LATER CAMBYSES DIED ON HIS WAY BACK FROM A VICTORIOUS CAMPAIGN IN EGYPT...

DARIUS I BECAME KING IN 522 BC ...

A YEAR LATER, IN JERUSALEM ...

THE WORK ON THE TEMPLE? I DON'T BELIEVE IN THAT ANY MORE!

HIS NAME IS HAGGAI.*

I DIDN'T EITHER! BUT YESTERDAY I HEARD A PROPHET ENCOURAGING US TO BEGIN WORK AGAIN...

GO UP INTO THE HILLS AND FETCH WOOD TO REBUILD THE TEMPLE. THEN I'LL BE GLAD AND I'LL BE GLORIFIED. THAT IS WHAT THE LORD SAYS.

* 'My festival'.

THEN I HAD ANOTHER VISION...

...AND THE MESSENGER SAID TO ME: 'THE SEVEN LAMPS ARE THE EYES OF GOD, WATCHING WHAT HAPPENS ON EARTH, AND THE TWO OLIVE-TREES ARE TWO MEN CHOSEN AND ANOINTED WITH OIL ...

... THEY SERVE THE LORD.'

ARE THEY ZERUBBABEL AND JOSHUA?

DOES THAT MEAN THAT THE TEMPLE WILL SOON BE FINISHED?

OTHER EXILES, WHO SHARED THE SAME HOPE, RETURNED FROM BABYLON.

WHEN THE LORD BROUGHT OUR CAPTIVES HOME, IT WAS LIKE A DREAM. HOW WE LAUGHED! HOW WE SANG FOR JOY! LORD, RESTORE OUR FORTUNES, LIKE STREAMS IN THE DESERT. LET THOSE WHO WEPT AS THEY SOWED THE SEED COME BACK SINGING FOR JOY, AS THEY GATHER IN THE HARVEST.

Psalm 126

NOW THE JEWS WERE SURE THAT KING DARIUS WAS ON THEIR SIDE. ENCOURAGED BY THEIR PROPHETS, THEY SET TO WORK ALL THE MORE EAGERLY...

...WHILE THE SAMARITANS WATCHED BITTERLY.

ARE WE GOING TO LEAVE THEM ALONE?

THIS TIME WE DON'T HAVE A CHOICE!

IN FACT KING DARIUS HAD THOUGHT OF EVERYTHING:

ANYONE WHO DISOBEYS MY ORDER IS TO BE HANGED ON A WOODEN BEAM PULLED OUT OF HIS HOUSE, AND HIS HOUSE WILL BE BROKEN DOWN.

THE WORK WAS FINISHED IN 515 BC.

WHAT ARE WE GOING TO PUT IN THE MOST HOLY PLACE? WE DON'T HAVE THE TABLETS OF THE LAW OR THE COVENANT BOX ANY LONGER...

NOW ALL WE HAVE TO DO IS TO PUT THE HOLY VESSELS IN THEIR PLACES.

WE'LL PUT THE STONE THERE!

THE STONE?

LORD, OUR GOD, BLESS THIS HOUSE, AND LET YOUR GLORY STAY HERE!

AMEN!

MAY THE LORD HEAR US!

THE LORD, OUR GOD!

MANY SACRIFICES WERE OFFERED ON THE ALTAR OF THE TEMPLE.

THE LEVITES TOOK UP THEIR WORK AGAIN...

BE FAITHFUL IN YOUR DUTY AND IN SAYING THE PRAYERS OF THE LORD'S HOUSE.

WHAT A FESTIVAL! I WOULDN'T HAVE MISSED IT FOR ALL THE WORLD!

YES! AFTER A DAY LIKE THIS, YOU'RE NOT SORRY YOU CAME BACK!

LIFE SLOWLY BECAME NORMAL AGAIN, AND, AS THE YEARS WENT BY, THE PEOPLE BECAME LESS KEEN.

WHAT ARE YOU DREAMING ABOUT, MALACHI?

I'M THINKING ABOUT MY FAMILY I LEFT IN BABYLON... ABOUT MY WIFE...

TOMORROW IT WILL BE TWENTY-FIVE YEARS!

YOU SHOULD HAVE MARRIED AGAIN HERE. PLENTY OF OTHERS DID...

BUT THE LAW OF MOSES FORBIDS IT!

SO WHAT? YOU HAVE TO LIVE... COME, LET US GO HOME.

WHEN I CAME TO THIS COUNTRY, I WAS ONLY A CHILD. MY MOTHER AND MY SISTERS WERE STILL IN BABYLON...

LATER ON I COULDN'T FIND AN ISRAELITE GIRL, SO I MARRIED A MOABITE.

...THAT'S ALSO FORBIDDEN IN THE LAW. BUT... WHAT IS TO BE DONE?

TURN BACK TO GOD BEFORE IT'S TOO LATE!

EARLY THE NEXT DAY MALACHI SET OUT FOR JERUSALEM.

I'LL FIND AN ANSWER TO ALL THESE QUESTIONS THERE...

WHEN HE REACHED JERUSALEM, MALACHI WENT UP TO THE TEMPLE.

I NEED TWO PIGEONS.

YOU'RE IN LUCK! MINE ARE THE BEST IN TOWN!

IS IT TRUE THAT SOME PRIESTS HAVE MARRIED WOMEN WHO AREN'T JEWISH?

YES! AND IT DIDN'T START YESTERDAY EITHER...

THEN KEEP YOUR PIGEONS! THE LORD WON'T ACCEPT SUCH SACRIFICES!

HE'S RIGHT! IT'S DISGRACEFUL!

COME WITH ME! I KNOW A GROUP OF PROPHETS WHO WILL BE GLAD TO WELCOME YOU...

LET ME INTRODUCE MY FRIEND, MALACHI.

MALACHI! THE LORD HAS CHOSEN YOU TO SPEAK TO HIS PEOPLE.

21

A SON KNOWS HIS FATHER, AND A SLAVE KNOWS HIS MASTER. THEN WHY DON'T YOU HONOUR ME AND RESPECT ME? THIS IS WHAT THE LORD SAYS.

AND YOU PRIESTS! YOUR TEACHING HAS MADE PEOPLE DO WRONG. YOU'VE BROKEN THE HOLY COVENANT!

I'LL SEND A CURSE UPON YOU, AND TURN YOUR BLESSINGS UPSIDE DOWN!

COME AWAY! WE DON'T NEED TO LET HIS WORDS DIRTY US.

IT IS ONLY THE ONE WHO SPEAKS THEM WHO GETS DIRTY!

MALACHI, YOU MUST KEEP ON. THE LORD'S SPIRIT IS ON YOU.

ONE DAY HE MET HIS FRIEND AGAIN IN THE STREETS OF JERUSALEM.

MALACHI, WHAT HAS HAPPENED TO YOU? YOU'VE CHANGED!

THE MEN OF JUDAH HAVE BROKEN THEIR PROMISE TO GOD BY MARRYING WOMEN WHO WORSHIP OTHER GODS.

I'LL SAY NO MORE! PRAY THAT THE LORD WILL HAVE MERCY ON US!

...HE'LL MAKE PEACE BETWEEN FATHERS AND THEIR CHILDREN, AND BETWEEN CHILDREN AND THEIR FATHERS.

THE GOVERNOR WILL BE INTERESTED IN WHAT HE IS SAYING.

RIGHT! LET'S GO!

IN THE PALACE OF THE GOVERNOR, ONE OF ZERUBBABEL'S SUCCESSORS...

MALACHI? WHO IS HE?

HE FINDS A GREAT DEAL OF FAULT WITH THE PRIESTS...

...AND TALKS ABOUT THE GREAT DAY OF THE LORD.

NOTHING VERY BAD ABOUT THAT! NOTHING VERY NEW, EITHER!

THE PERSIANS GIVE ME MORE TROUBLE THAN THESE POOR PROPHETS!

WHAT DO YOU MEAN, SIR?

KING DARIUS IS VERY ILL; HIS REIGN WILL SOON BE OVER...

JERUSALEM

REBUILT BY EZRA AND NEHEMIAH

EZRA, the scribe

THE FIRST JEWS HAD GONE BACK TO JUDAH FROM BABYLON IN 538 B.C. THEY HAD BEEN ABLE TO FINISH REBUILDING THE TEMPLE IN 515. BUT, AS THE YEARS PASSED, THE PEOPLE QUARRELLED WITH ONE ANOTHER, AND THEY DID NOT OBEY THE LAW OF MOSES.

THIS WORRIED THE FAITHFUL JEWS WHO WERE STILL IN BABYLON. SO **EZRA** THE SCRIBE WENT TO THE KING...

MASTER EZRA!

WELL, WHAT DID THE KING SAY?

SCENARIO: Etienne DAHLER
DRAWING: Victor de la FUENTE

KING ARTAXERXES THOUGHT DEEPLY ABOUT YOUR REQUEST, BUT...

BUT WHAT?

BEFORE MAKING A DECISION, HE WOULD LIKE TO STUDY YOUR... LAW IN DETAIL.

THE TORAH! TELL HIM I'LL LET HIM HAVE IT SOON.

SO EZRA COLLECTED THE DIFFERENT SCROLLS WHICH MADE UP THE TORAH.

THEN ARTAXERXES STUDIED THE PRECIOUS SCROLLS FOR HIMSELF.

AMAZING! THIS LITTLE NATION IS REALLY CLEVER!

A LITTLE WHILE LATER, **EZRA** WAS CALLED TO THE PALACE.

JUST A FEW MORE STEPS TO CLIMB, REUBEN, AND WE'LL KNOW MORE ABOUT WHAT IS GOING TO HAPPEN TO ISRAEL!

YOUR LAW DOESN'T GO AGAINST OURS AT ANY POINT. SO I'VE DECIDED THAT IT WILL BE THE LAW IN THE LAND OF JUDAH.

STANDING BEFORE KING ARTAXERXES...

MASTER EZRA, I GIVE YOU FULL AUTHORITY TO GOVERN BY IT!

27

NO PRIESTS? BUT THAT'S DISGRACEFUL!

YOU MUST UNDERSTAND! HERE IN BABYLON THEY CAN GROW RICH. THERE IN JUDAH THEY'LL HAVE NO LAND; THEY'LL HAVE TO LIVE ON WHAT OTHER PEOPLE GIVE THEM, SO THEY'LL ALWAYS BE POOR!

SOMEHOW THEY MANAGED TO PERSUADE SOME LEVITES TO JOIN THE GROUP.

BUT, EZRA, WE CAN'T LEAVE WITHOUT AN ESCORT... IT'S MADNESS!

WHY DID YOU REFUSE THE BODY-GUARD THE KING OFFERED US?

I WOULD HAVE BEEN ASHAMED TO ACCEPT IT, BECAUSE I HAD TOLD HIM THAT GOD WOULD PROTECT US.

EZRA ASKED HIS COMPANIONS TO FAST AND PRAY FOR GOD'S BLESSING.

PERHAPS I WAS WRONG, BUT WE MUST TRUST THE ALMIGHTY GOD.

HOW SHALL WE EVER GET TO JERUSALEM SAFE AND SOUND?

29

A LIST WAS MADE OF EVERYTHING THE RICH JEWISH FAMILIES AND KING ARTAXERXES HIMSELF HAD GIVEN.

EACH ONE OF YOU MUST LOOK AFTER ONE THING, UNTIL WE REACH JERUSALEM.

AT LAST THE GROUP SET OFF.

BE BRAVE! THE LORD IS LOOKING AFTER US!

THEY PRESSED ON. THERE WAS NO TROUBLE FROM BRIGANDS OR ROBBERS.

AFTER TRAVELLING FOR 5 MONTHS...

JERUSALEM!

PRAISE THE LORD!

WE'VE ARRIVED!

BROTHER, THERE IS JERUSALEM!

31

AFTER SOME MONTHS...

EZRA SENT MESSENGERS THROUGHOUT JUDAH.

HEY, SIMEON, HAVE YOU HEARD THE NEWS?

WHAT?

ALL THE JEWS IN THE PROVINCE ARE ORDERED TO GO TO JERUSALEM... AND IF YOU WON'T GO...

...ALL YOUR PROPERTY WILL BE SEIZED, AND YOU'LL BE SHUT OUT OF THE COMMUNITY!

VERY WELL! MY WOOD WILL HAVE TO WAIT!

GROUPS CAME TO JERUSALEM FROM ALL OVER JUDAH.

IF YOU ASK ME, THEY HAVEN'T CALLED US HERE TO GIVE US PRIZES!

IN FACT, EZRA WAS DOING ALL HE COULD TO MAKE HIS PEOPLE RESPECT THE LAW OF MOSES.

MEN OF ISRAEL, YOU'VE DONE WRONG BY MARRYING FOREIGN WOMEN! IT IS HIGH TIME YOU TURNED BACK TO GOD. GET RID OF ALL YOUR WIVES WHO AREN'T JEWISH!

ALMOST EVERYBODY DID WHAT EZRA ORDERED.

EZRA ALSO MADE HIS HARSH ORDER A LITTLE SOFTER...

THE LEADING MEN OF THE TOWNS AND VILLAGES WILL COME TOGETHER TO EXAMINE EACH CASE.

A FEW DAYS LATER THOSE WHO WERE GUILTY APPEARED BEFORE THEIR JUDGES.

MY WIFE IS A CANAANITE WHO HAS NO FAMILY. IF I DIVORCE HER, SHE'LL STARVE TO DEATH, OR ELSE SHE'LL HAVE TO BECOME A PROSTITUTE!

FROM TODAY SHE IS NO LONGER YOUR WIFE... BUT KEEP HER IN YOUR HOME, AND LOOK AFTER HER.

I'LL DO THAT, I PROMISE!

IN THREE MONTHS ALL MARRIAGES WITH FOREIGN WOMEN WERE ENDED.

NEHEMIAH
the reformer

YOU SEE; MY BROTHER NEHEMIAH LIVES UP THERE NEAR THE KING'S PALACE.

WHAT A SPLENDID CITY!

SOME YEARS PASSED... IN 445 BC A SMALL GROUP OF JEWS FROM JERUSALEM ARRIVED IN THE CITY OF SUSA. (THE THREE PERSIAN CAPITALS WERE SUSA, BABYLON, AND ECBATANA.)

HANANI! MY BROTHER! GOD BE PRAISED!

NEHEMIAH, I'M SO GLAD TO SEE YOU AGAIN! IT'S A LONG WAY FROM JERUSALEM TO SUSA!

COME AND REST. WE'LL TALK LATER!

WHAT IS YOUR NEWS?

NEHEMIAH, THINGS AREN'T GOOD! JERUSALEM HAS NO WALL TO DEFEND IT... ANYBODY COULD CAPTURE IT AT ANY TIME...

SO WHAT HAS EZRA BEEN DOING?

HE HAS PUT THE RELIGIOUS THINGS RIGHT, BUT IS THAT ENOUGH?

WE NEED A STRONG CITY THAT CAN STAND AGAINST THE THREATS OF OUR ENEMIES.

THE KING IS WAITING FOR ME. I MUST GO BACK TO THE PALACE. I'LL SEE YOU IN THE MORNING.

...REBUILD THE WALLS... REORGANIZE JERUSALEM... BUT HOW?

SO NEHEMIAH FASTED, AND PUT HIS TRUST IN GOD...

LORD, HELP ME! FOR THE LOVE OF YOUR PEOPLE...

A LITTLE WHILE LATER, IN THE KING'S PALACE...

NEHEMIAH, YOU LOOK WORRIED... YOU'RE NOT ILL... SO WHAT IS IT?

YOUR MAJESTY, HOW CAN I BE HAPPY WHEN THE CITY OF MY FATHERS IS IN RUINS?

BUT... THE TEMPLE HAS BEEN REBUILT...

YES, YOUR MAJESTY, BUT THE WALLS ARE BROKEN DOWN AND THE CITY GATES ARE SMASHED.

SO WHAT DO YOU WANT?

SEND ME TO JUDAH TO REBUILD JERUSALEM! AFTER THAT I'LL COME BACK.

VERY WELL... BUT COME BACK SOON!

AT THE END OF THE YEAR 445 BC, NEHEMIAH LEFT SUSA, WITH LETTERS GIVING ORDERS FOR THE WALLS OF THE HOLY CITY TO BE REBUILT.

NEHEMIAH'S THOROUGH INSPECTION LET HIM SEE IN WHAT A BAD STATE THE CITY WALLS WERE.

* Until then it had been under the Governor of Samaria.

THE WORK QUICKLY WENT AHEAD. THE NEWS REACHED **SANBALLAT**, GOVERNOR OF THE PROVINCE OF SAMARIA, AND **TOBIAH**, GOVERNOR OF THE PROVINCE OF AMMON.

THE JEWS HAVE STOLEN JUDAH FROM ME, AND NOW THEY JEER AT ME FROM THE TOP OF THEIR WALLS!

COME, COME! LET THEM CARRY ON! A FOX COULD JUMP OVER THEIR WALLS!

WE'RE HALF WAY!

YES, WE'VE DONE THE HARDEST PART.

THIS TROUBLED THE PROVINCES AROUND JUDAH.
SANBALLAT FORMED AN ALLIANCE TO ATTACK JERUSALEM.

TAKE THEM BY SURPRISE; KILL THEM; AND THEN GET AWAY!

SUSA MUSTN'T KNOW WHO MADE THE ATTACK!

BUT, WHEN THEY ARRIVED UNDER THE WALLS OF JERUSALEM, IT WAS THEY WHO WERE SURPRISED.

HAVE FAITH IN THE LORD, AND REMEMBER: YOU'RE FIGHTING FOR YOUR BROTHERS AND CHILDREN!

WHAT IS GOING ON?

WAIT...

THERE, ON THE WALLS... THEY'RE ARMED!

THERE ARE MANY OF THEM!

LET'S GO! THIS IS TOO RISKY!

I CAN SEE A GROUP!

THE ENEMY GAVE UP THE IDEA OF ATTACKING JERUSALEM.

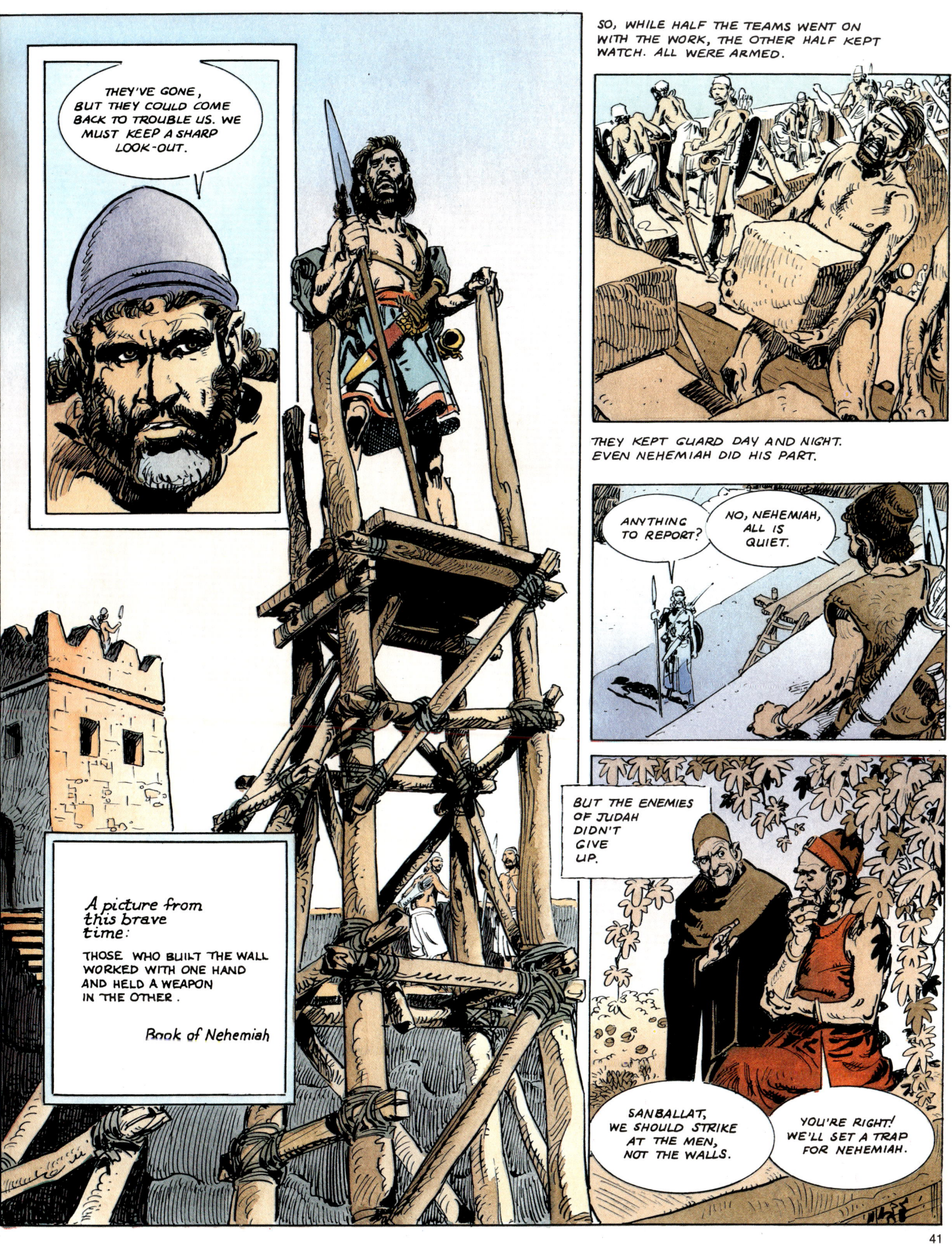

SO, WHILE HALF THE TEAMS WENT ON WITH THE WORK, THE OTHER HALF KEPT WATCH. ALL WERE ARMED.

THEY'VE GONE, BUT THEY COULD COME BACK TO TROUBLE US. WE MUST KEEP A SHARP LOOK-OUT.

THEY KEPT GUARD DAY AND NIGHT. EVEN NEHEMIAH DID HIS PART.

ANYTHING TO REPORT?

NO, NEHEMIAH, ALL IS QUIET.

A picture from this brave time:

THOSE WHO BUILT THE WALL WORKED WITH ONE HAND AND HELD A WEAPON IN THE OTHER.

Book of Nehemiah

BUT THE ENEMIES OF JUDAH DIDN'T GIVE UP.

SANBALLAT, WE SHOULD STRIKE AT THE MEN, NOT THE WALLS.

YOU'RE RIGHT! WE'LL SET A TRAP FOR NEHEMIAH.

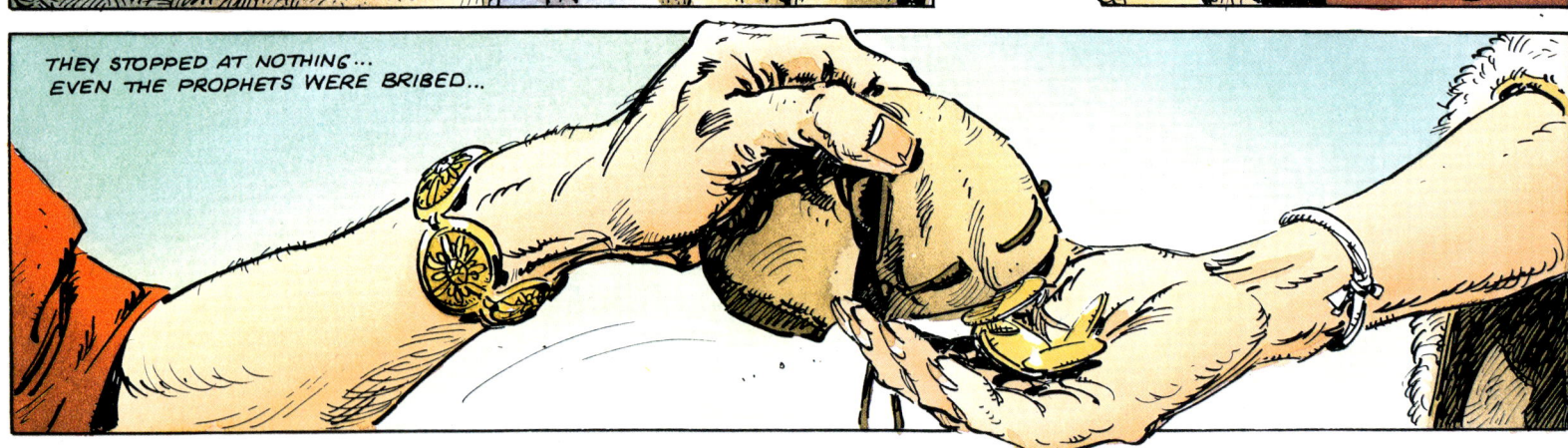

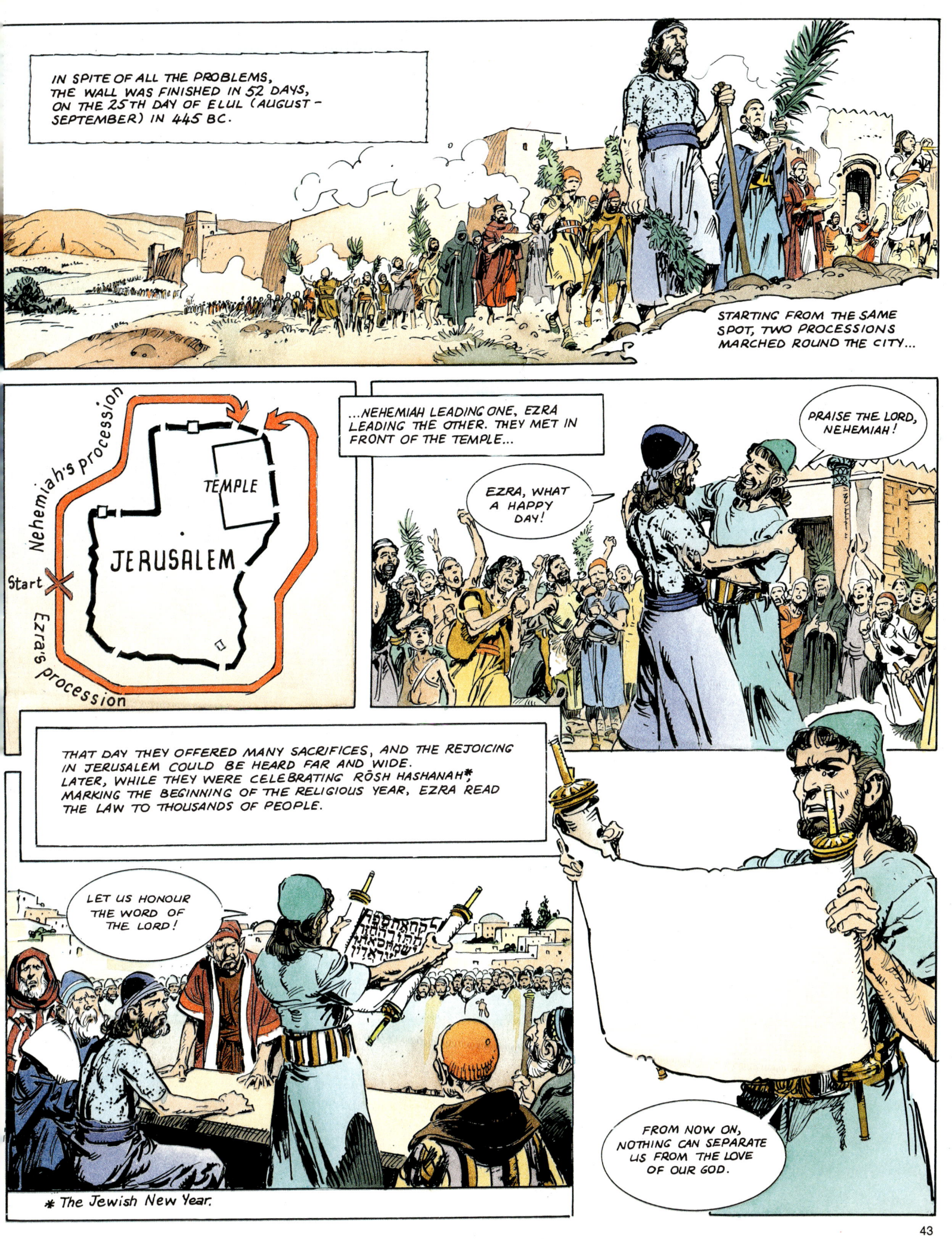

IN SPITE OF ALL THE PROBLEMS, THE WALL WAS FINISHED IN 52 DAYS, ON THE 25TH DAY OF ELUL (AUGUST — SEPTEMBER) IN 445 B.C.

STARTING FROM THE SAME SPOT, TWO PROCESSIONS MARCHED ROUND THE CITY...

Nehemiah's procession

Start ✗

Ezra's procession

TEMPLE

JERUSALEM

...NEHEMIAH LEADING ONE, EZRA LEADING THE OTHER. THEY MET IN FRONT OF THE TEMPLE...

EZRA, WHAT A HAPPY DAY!

PRAISE THE LORD, NEHEMIAH!

THAT DAY THEY OFFERED MANY SACRIFICES, AND THE REJOICING IN JERUSALEM COULD BE HEARD FAR AND WIDE. LATER, WHILE THEY WERE CELEBRATING ROSH HASHANAH*, MARKING THE BEGINNING OF THE RELIGIOUS YEAR, EZRA READ THE LAW TO THOUSANDS OF PEOPLE.

LET US HONOUR THE WORD OF THE LORD!

FROM NOW ON, NOTHING CAN SEPARATE US FROM THE LOVE OF OUR GOD.

* The Jewish New Year.

43

THEN CAME SUKKOTH, THE FESTIVAL OF SHELTERS. THEY THANKED THE ETERNAL GOD FOR PROVIDING ALL THAT HIS PEOPLE NEEDED.

HURRY UP, BENJAMIN! WE'LL NEVER BE FINISHED!

DON'T WORRY, DAD! OUR SUKKAH* WILL BE READY TONIGHT. I'M SURE IT WILL BE THE BEST!

*Shelter.

THEY ATE AND SLEPT IN THE SHELTER FOR A WEEK.

THIS IS WHAT IT WILL BE LIKE WHEN WE SHARE GOD'S HOME! OUR JOY WILL NEVER END!

TWO DAYS AFTER SUKKOTH, EZRA AND NEHEMIAH CALLED THE PEOPLE TOGETHER AGAIN FOR A DAY OF PRAYER AND FASTING.

NOW WE'RE GOING TO MAKE OUR COVENANT WITH THE LORD AGAIN.

SO THE REPRESENTATIVES OF THE PEOPLE CAME FORWARD AND SIGNED THE AGREEMENT IN WHICH THEY PROMISED TO LIVE BY THE LAW OF MOSES.

HANANI, MY BROTHER, I WANT YOU TO TAKE CHARGE OF JERUSALEM...

YOUR WISHES ARE MY ORDERS, NEHEMIAH!

DO YOUR BEST TO REBUILD THE PARTS OF THE CITY STILL IN RUINS, AND BRING MORE PEOPLE TO LNE IN IT.

I'LL DO THAT.

IN EACH TOWN AND VILLAGE OF THE PROVINCE THEY GATHERED THE PEOPLE INTO GROUPS OF TEN. THEN...

YOU'VE DRAWN THE BLACK PEBBLE. JOSEPH MUST GO AND LIVE IN JERUSALEM!

VOLUNTEERS JOINED THOSE WHO WERE CHOSEN BY LOT TO LIVE IN THE CITY.

I'VE HAD TO LEAVE MY FIELDS... I WONDER HOW I'LL BE ABLE TO KEEP MY FAMILY.

BAH! YOU'LL BECOME A TRADER!

AT LEAST WE'LL BE SAFE BEHIND THE WALLS.

EVERY EVENING THE GATES WERE SHUT AT SUNSET, AND NOT OPENED AGAIN UNTIL DAWN.

ONCE HE HAD FINISHED REBUILDING JERUSALEM, NEHEMIAH COULD DEAL WITH THINGS WHICH NEEDED TO BE PUT RIGHT.

A BAD HARVEST... AND I'LL HAVE TO BORROW TO PAY MY TAXES!

...I'VE BEEN HERE TWO YEARS, AND I'VE NOTHING LEFT!

AND TO THINK THEY'RE JEWS WHO TREAT US LIKE THIS!

IF WE ARE THE LORD'S PEOPLE, WE SHOULD BEHAVE DIFFERENTLY!

NEHEMIAH, HELP US! I BEG YOU!

NEHEMIAH TOOK STRONG ACTION. HE CALLED ALL THE RICH PEOPLE TOGETHER.

I'VE FOUND OUT THAT YOU'RE DRIVING YOUR OWN BROTHERS INTO SLAVERY. YOU LET THEM DIE OF HUNGER, WHILE YOU HAVE PLENTY TO EAT!

WE CAN'T HAVE THAT! IN THE NAME OF THE LORD, I COMMAND YOU TO STOP!

WE'RE BEING FORCED TO CANCEL ALL DEBTS... TO GIVE BACK FIELDS AND VINEYARDS...

I DON'T THINK NEHEMIAH IS GIVING US A CHOICE.

AS THE YEARS WENT BY, NEHEMIAH CARRIED ON HIS WORK. HE GOVERNED THE PROVINCE WISELY AND WELL, AND EVERYBODY RESPECTED HIM.

THERE'S A FINE MAN! NO ONE CAN CRITICIZE HIM.

YES, HE HAS NEVER IMPOSED THE TAXES TO WHICH HE HAS THE RIGHT AS GOVERNOR.

IN THE CITY, JEWS WHO WERE FAITHFUL TO GOD MET TO STUDY THE LAW.

AFTER THAT I'LL SEND MY SPIRIT ON ALL PEOPLE. YOUR SONS AND YOUR DAUGHTERS WILL PROCLAIM MY MESSAGE; YOUR OLD MEN WILL DREAM DREAMS, AND YOUR YOUNG MEN WILL SEE VISIONS...

WORDS RECENTLY SPOKEN BY THE PROPHET JOEL.

AT THAT TIME I WILL POUR OUT MY SPIRIT EVEN ON SLAVES, MEN AND WOMEN.

I WILL GIVE SIGNS IN THE SKY AND ON THE EARTH, BEFORE THE GREAT AND TERRIBLE DAY OF THE LORD COMES.

THEN ALL WHO ASK THE LORD FOR HELP WILL BE SAVED. THEY WILL LIVE IN JERUSALEM FOR EVER. I'LL LEAVE NOTHING UNPUNISHED, BECAUSE I'LL LIVE IN ZION FOR EVER.

SOME PEOPLE THOUGHT THE DARK DAYS ANNOUNCED BY JOEL WERE NEAR...

FOR MY PART, HANANI, I DON'T THINK SO, AND I'M GOING BACK TO SUSA, AS I PLANNED.

NEHEMIAH, I WON'T STOP YOU. I KNOW THE KING IS WAITING FOR YOU.

YES, HE'S BEEN WAITING ELEVEN YEARS FOR ME!

FAREWELL, JERUSALEM!

BUT NEHEMIAH WOULD COME BACK SOME YEARS LATER, TO SETTLE CERTAIN QUARRELS, AND PUT AN END TO SOME OF THE WRONG THINGS THE PEOPLE WERE DOING.

FROM NOW ON JERUSALEM WOULD BE THE HEART OF GOD'S PEOPLE, THE HOLY CITY TO WHICH THEY LOVED TO GO ON PILGRIMAGE.

I WAS GLAD WHEN THEY SAID TO ME, 'LET US GO TO THE LORD'S HOUSE.' AND NOW WE'RE HERE, STANDING INSIDE THE GATES OF JERUSALEM.

Psalm 122